T0389969

CHEMISTRY EXPLAINED

CHEMISTRY IN THE LAB & NATURE

by
Janet Bingham

Minneapolis, Minnesota

Credits
Cover and title page, © Olga Yastremska/Adobe Stock Images; 4T, © Science History Images/Alamy Stock PhotoK; 4B, © Jack Jeffries/Adobe Stock Images; 4–5, © SDI Productions/iStock; 5, © marritch_2020/Adobe Stock Images; 6T, © firatturgut /Shutterstock; 6M, © twixx/Adobe Stock Images; 6B, © Science History Institute/Wikimedia Commons; 6–7, © Ground Picture/Shutterstock; 7, © Ann Bulashenko/Shutterstock; 8, © OSweetNature/Shutterstock; 8–9, © DeepSkyTX/Shutterstock; 9T, © Smithsonian Institution/Wikimedia Commons; 9B, © Ad_hominem/Shutterstock; 10T, © Photoongraphy/Shutterstock; 10B, © VectorMine/Shutterstock; 10–11, © DoJed YeT/Shutterstock; 11, © CrutchDerm2014/Wikimedia Commons; 12T, © VectorMine/Shutterstock; 12B, © CrutchDerm2014/Wikimedia Commons; 12–13, © Francesco ConT/Shutterstock; 13, © Vladimir Arndt/Shutterstock; 14T, © Kichigin/Shutterstock; 14M, © Merkushev Vasiliy/Shutterstock; 14B, © CrutchDerm2014/Wikimedia Commons; 14–15, © Dragos AsaWei/Shutterstock; 15, © Maleo/Shutterstock; 16T, © GraphicsRF.com/Shutterstock; 16B, © Peter Gudella/Shutterstock; 16–17, © Vitaliy Karimov/Shutterstock; 17, © /Welcome Collection; 18T, © Seqoya/Shutterstock; 18B, © VectorMine/Shutterstock; 18–19, © Melissa Burovac/Shutterstock; 19, © Ellen Sharples/Wikimedia Commons; 20T, © petrroudny43/Shutterstock; 20B, © Dark Moon Pictures/Shutterstock; 20–21, © TinaSova20/Shutterstock; 21, © Public Domain/Wikimedia Commons; 22T, © Science History Images/Alamy Stock Photo; 22B, © Archive PL/Alamy Stock Photo; 22–23, © hutch photography/Shutterstock; 23, © DKN0049/Shutterstock; 24T, © LillieGraphie/Shutterstock; 24B, © ju_see/Shutterstock; 24–25, © Nick Upton/Nature Picture Library; 25, © Bearport Publishing; 26T, © ShadeDesign/Shutterstock; 26B, © Beautiful landscape/Shutterstock; 26–27, © winnond/Shutterstock; 27, © Bearport Publishing; 28T, © pintoreduardo/Adobe Stock Images; 28B, © Ertugrul Sucu/Adobe Stock Images; 28–29, © S. Singha/Adobe Stock Images; 29, © University of Bristol/Wikimedia Commons; 30T, © chromatos/Shutterstock; 30B, © Biology Education/Shutterstock; 30–31, © New Africa/Adobe Stock Images; 31T, © SCIENCE SOURCE/Science Photo Library; 31B, © Science History Institute/Wikimedia Commons; 32T, © SCIENCE SOURCE/Science Photo Library; 32B, © SCIENCE SOURCE/Science Photo Library; 32–33, © Rafya Thongdumhyu/Shutterstock and © Inkoly/Shutterstock and © Bjoern Wylezich/Shutterstock, 33, © SCIENCE SOURCE/Science Photo Library; 34T, © Steve Cymro/Shutterstock; 34B, © denisk0/Getty Images; 34–35, © SCIENCE SOURCE/Science Photo Library; 35, © i viewfinder/Shutterstock; 36T, © Nandalal Sarkar/Shutterstock; 36M, © fabio/Adobe Stock Images; 36B, © MARTYN F. CHILLMAID/Science Photo Library; 36–37, © Guitar photographer/Shutterstock; 37, © Huangdan2060/Wikimedia Commons; 38T, © TarTla/Shutterstock; 38M, © MoFarouk/Shutterstock; 38B, © University of Bristol/Wikimedia Commons; 38–39, © S.Borisov/Shutterstock; 39TL, © nd700/Adobe Stock Images; 39BR, © Cergios/Shutterstock; 40T, © zcxes/Shutterstock; 40B, © PEGGY GREB / US DEPARTMENT OF AGRICULTURE/Science Photo Library; 40–41, © DonSmith/Alamy Stock Photo; 41, © Letizia Mancino Cremer/Wikimedia Commons; 42, © SINITAR/Shutterstock; 42–43, © shironosov/iStock; 43, © petert2/Adobe Stock Images; 44, © Tartila/Shutterstock; 45T, © DKN0049/Shutterstock; 45B, © SCIENCE SOURCE/Science Photo Library; 47, © Melissa Burovac/Shutterstock

Bearport Publishing Company Product Development Team
Publisher: Jen Jenson; Director of Product Development: Spencer Brinker; Editorial Director: Allison Juda; Editor: Cole Nelson; Editor: Tiana Tran; Production Editor: Naomi Reich; Art Director: Kim Jones; Designer: Kayla Eggert; Designer: Steve Scheluchin; Production Specialist: Owen Hamlin

Statement on Usage of Generative Artificial Intelligence
Bearport Publishing remains committed to publishing high-quality nonfiction books. Therefore, we restrict the use of generative AI to ensure accuracy of all text and visual components pertaining to a book's subject. See BearportPublishing.com for details.

Library of Congress Cataloging-in-Publication Data is available at www.loc.gov or upon request from the publisher.

ISBN: 979-8-89577-496-0 (hardcover)
ISBN: 979-8-89577-538-7 (paperback)
ISBN: 979-8-89577-504-2 (ebook)

© 2026 Arcturus Holdings Limited. This edition is published by arrangement with Arcturus Publishing Limited.

North American adaptations © 2026 Bearport Publishing Company. All rights reserved. No part of this publication may be reproduced in whole or in part, stored in any retrieval system, or transmitted in any form or by any means, electronic, mechanical, photocopying, recording, or otherwise, without written permission from the publisher. Bearport Publishing is a division of FlutterBee Education Group.

For more information, write to Bearport Publishing, 3500 American Blvd W, Suite 150, Bloomington, MN 55431.

Contents

The World Is Chemistry 4
Chemists at Work 6
The First Chemicals 8
Earth Chemistry 10
Rocks and Minerals 12
Wonderful Water 14
Creative Carbon 16
Essential Oxygen 18
Team Nitrogen 20
Crucial Glucose 22
Plant Chemicals 24
Body Chemistry 26
Chemists in the Lab 28
Reagents 30
Acid and Alkali Tests 32
Acid Reactions 34
Fire and Flame Tests 36
Spectra 38
Chromatography 40
Learning from Nature 42

Review and Reflect 44
Glossary 46
Read More 47
Learn More Online 47
Index 48

The World Is Chemistry

Chemistry happens all around us. From the changing colors of leaves in the woods to bubbling experiments at a science fair, chemicals are constantly interacting, combining, and separating in strange and interesting ways. This often changes chemicals into new substances with very different properties. Chemists study chemicals out in nature as well as in scientific laboratories.

Chemistry throughout History

Chemists have been studying chemicals and how they react to one another for thousands of years. They first made discoveries by observing changes in nature. Later, they built tools to separate or combine chemicals to learn about their properties. These tools became part of the first chemical labs.

Chemistry in Nature

Living things in nature use many chemical processes to get the energy or nutrients they need from the world. In plants, the process of photosynthesis uses sunlight to turn the gas carbon dioxide into the sugar glucose and the gas oxygen. Animals use respiration to create energy using oxygen, turning that oxygen into carbon dioxide.

From Nature to the Lab and Back

Many chemists closely study chemical processes in nature to learn if they can be applied to new uses. For example, chemists have recently learned how to create synthetic proteins called enzymes. These enzymes, usually found only in living things, can help scientists pull nitrogen out of the air to create fertilizers that help plants grow.

Chemists at Work

Chemists investigate what chemicals are made of and what properties they have. The simplest of these are the elements that make up all matter in the universe. Elements combine to make compounds with different properties.

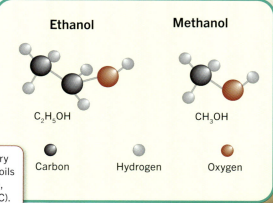

Two similar chemicals can have very different properties. Pure ethanol boils at 173 degrees Fahrenheit (78°C), while methanol boils at 149°F (65°C).

Melting and Boiling Points

Most matter exists in one of three states—solid, liquid, or gas—with things changing states as they get hotter or colder. We know the temperatures at which pure chemicals change state. These are called melting points and boiling points. If other chemicals are added, however, melting and boiling points change. These extra chemicals are called impurities. So, one way to see whether chemicals are pure is by checking their boiling points.

Pure water freezes at 32°F (0°C). Impurities lower the freezing point. Salt sprinkled on icy roads helps ice melt at colder temperatures.

HALL OF FAME

Marie Meurdrac
1610–1680

Marie Meurdrac was a French alchemist who wrote *Useful and Easy Chemistry, for the Benefit of Ladies*. She taught herself the principles of chemistry by reading about other people's experiments and setting up her own lab. Her book contained recipes for cosmetics and medicines, and it focused on low-cost treatments that could help the poor.

The Scientific Method

Scientists follow the same basic procedures when they do any experiment. First, they plan the experiment and predict the results. This prediction is called a hypothesis. Then, they do the experiment, carefully taking measurements to be sure their information is correct. Good scientists then repeat the tests to be sure their results are precise. Afterward, they write what they found out in a conclusion.

Glass thermometers should be read at eye level. Looking at them from above or below can cause an error in the reading.

A water molecule is a compound of one oxygen atom and two hydrogen atoms, chemically combined. Pure water boils at 212°F (100°C).

Digital thermometers are often safer to use than glass thermometers and may give more accurate results.

Tap water is considered an impure chemical because compounds other than water are dissolved in it. The impurities make the water boil at a higher temperature than pure water.

DID YOU KNOW? Helium has the lowest boiling point of all the elements. It changes from liquid to gas at a very chilly −452°F (−269°C).

The First Chemicals

The leading theory about how the universe began is the big bang theory. This states that 13.8 billion years ago, space was very small and so full of energy that it burst in a huge, hot explosion from which the universe is still expanding. The accuracy of this theory is supported by what we can detect from the elements across the universe.

Star Birth

By studying the light given off by stars such as the sun, scientists can tell that they are 99.9 percent hydrogen and helium—the lightest atoms in the universe. They first formed after the big bang and gathered into gas clouds, which later collapsed to make protostars. These were balls of hot gas containing hydrogen ions, or hydrogen atoms holding an electric charge. Nuclear fusion began to join the nuclei of hydrogen ions together to make helium, giving off the first starlight in the process.

The Forging of Elements

Nuclear fusion deep in the sun's core turns hydrogen into helium and produces energy. As a star ages, its core runs out of hydrogen fuel and starts fusing helium instead. Then, when helium fuel runs out, the nuclei of larger atoms start to fuse and produce heavier elements. When the star's core runs out of fuel, it collapses. As a giant star reaches the end of its life, its fuel becomes the heaviest elements in the universe before being scattered in a supernova explosion.

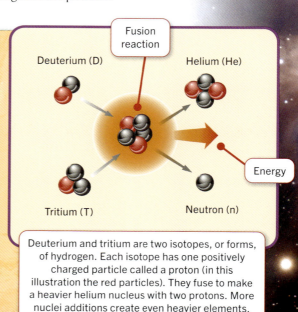

Deuterium and tritium are two isotopes, or forms, of hydrogen. Each isotope has one positively charged particle called a proton (in this illustration the red particles). They fuse to make a heavier helium nucleus with two protons. More nuclei additions create even heavier elements.

DID YOU KNOW? Nuclear fusion happens in new stars at temperatures greater than 27,000,000°F (15,000,000°C).

HALL OF FAME

Cecilia Payne-Gaposchkin
1900—1979

Astronomer and astrophysicist Cecilia Payne-Gaposchkin studied at Cambridge University in the United Kingdom. However, as a woman, she was not allowed to receive a degree at the time. She later became the first woman to earn a doctorate degree in astronomy from Radcliffe College in the United States. She discovered that the sun's light spectrum had far more hydrogen and helium than other elements and realized that hydrogen was the most abundant element in stars.

Galaxies are groups of stars that orbit a common center. They also contain gas and dust clouds called nebulae, where stars are born.

The Horsehead Nebula is 1,600 light-years away. That means its light takes 1,600 years to reach Earth.

The Orion constellation looks like a hunter with a bow.

Stars are chemical factories. Except for a few basic elements, such as hydrogen and helium, all the atoms in the universe were made inside stars.

We are all made of star stuff! Our atoms were formed in stars billions of years ago.

9

Earth Chemistry

Our solar system formed 4.6 billion years ago from a cloud of dust and gas around the sun. Near the hot center, dust gathered into rocks, and those rocks collided and clumped together. This eventually formed the rocky planets, including Earth. The molten materials inside these planets arranged themselves into layers. Heavier elements sank to form the cores, and lighter materials floated upward, cooled, and hardened into the crusts.

Young Earth

As Earth cooled, blocks of solid rock floating on molten rock became the crust. Volcanoes erupted, releasing gas elements that began to form the atmosphere. When Earth had cooled to below water's boiling point, water in the atmosphere condensed and began a rainstorm that lasted for centuries. Rain from this storm gathered in hollows on the surface and made the first oceans. Today, Earth's crust is still actively changing. It moves in huge tectonic plates and recycles itself through volcanic activity.

As the moon orbits Earth, its gravity pulls on the oceans, making tides. Tides drive ocean currents, which move warm water around the planet and help keep Earth's climate stable.

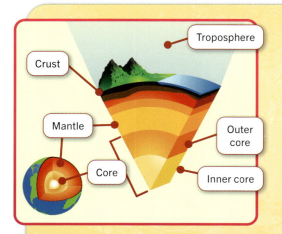

Layers of Earth

Earth has a solid inner core of iron and nickel surrounded by a liquid outer core. The layer above the core is called the mantle. It is made of hot, slowly flowing, semi-molten rock called magma. The crust above that is the outer layer of solid rock. We live on top of Earth's crust. Above us are the gases of the atmosphere, with the layer closest to the crust called the troposphere.

DID YOU KNOW? The moon's surface contains anorthosite—a rock also found on Earth. This suggests that parts of the moon may have once been part of Earth.

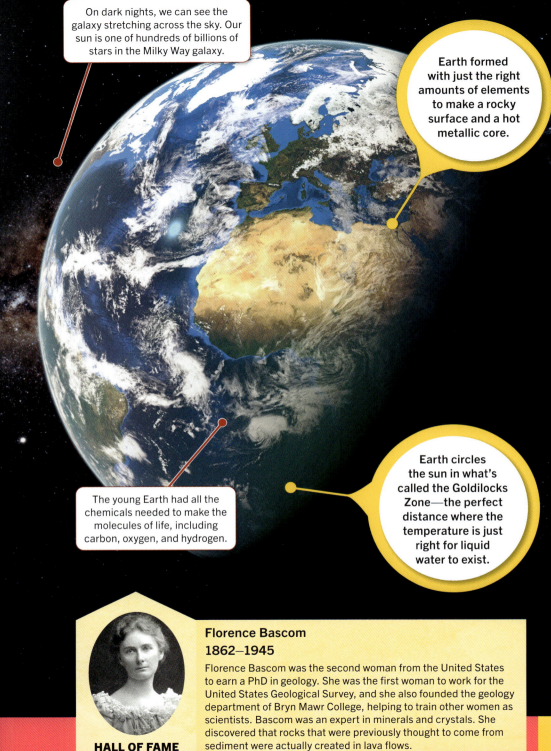

On dark nights, we can see the galaxy stretching across the sky. Our sun is one of hundreds of billions of stars in the Milky Way galaxy.

Earth formed with just the right amounts of elements to make a rocky surface and a hot metallic core.

The young Earth had all the chemicals needed to make the molecules of life, including carbon, oxygen, and hydrogen.

Earth circles the sun in what's called the Goldilocks Zone—the perfect distance where the temperature is just right for liquid water to exist.

HALL OF FAME

Florence Bascom
1862–1945

Florence Bascom was the second woman from the United States to earn a PhD in geology. She was the first woman to work for the United States Geological Survey, and she also founded the geology department of Bryn Mawr College, helping to train other women as scientists. Bascom was an expert in minerals and crystals. She discovered that rocks that were previously thought to come from sediment were actually created in lava flows.

Rocks and Minerals

Earth's crust is composed of elements and compounds combined into minerals that are mixed together in rocks. The crust is recycled over many thousands of years. Its rocks are pulled underground and back up to the surface by movements of the crust and by volcanic activity.

The Rock Cycle

Rocks move through Earth in the rock cycle. Sometimes, rocks get broken and worn down—or weathered—by forces such as moving water or wind. Then, they are carried away through erosion. These rocks may be carried to the sea where they fall to the bottom as sediment. The weight of rock and water above squashes them, forming solid sedimentary rocks. Rocks buried very deep, surrounded by high temperatures and pressure, change into metamorphic rocks. When metamorphic rocks are heated until they melt, that molten rock, or magma, comes to the surface in volcanoes and cools as igneous rocks.

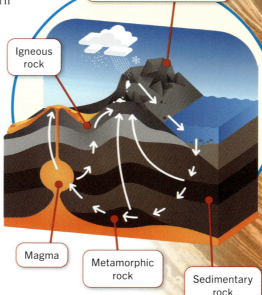

Rocks lifted to the surface are weathered and eroded.

Igneous rock

Magma

Metamorphic rock

Sedimentary rock

HALL OF FAME

Marie le Jars de Gournay
1565–1645

Marie le Jars de Gournay was a writer and early feminist. She argued for gender equality, insisting that women should have the same education and work rights as men. She performed practical experiments using alchemy, mineralogy, and philosophy.

12

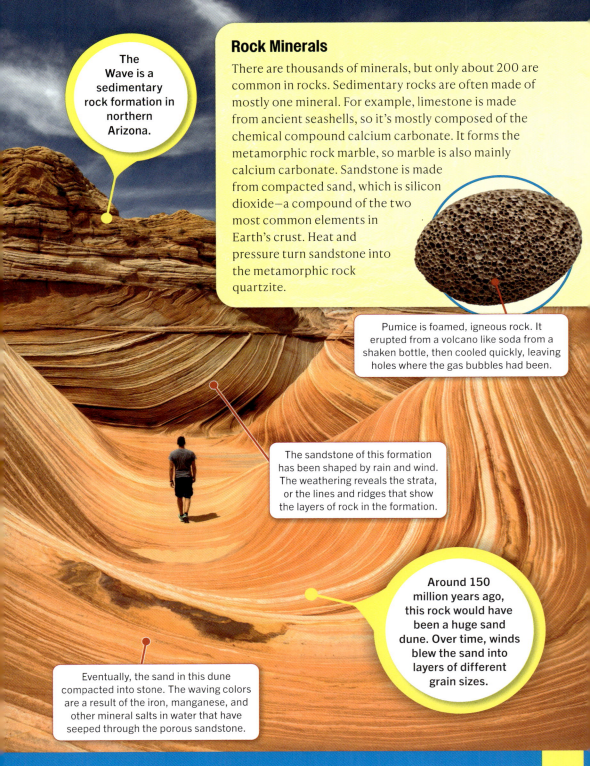

The Wave is a sedimentary rock formation in northern Arizona.

Rock Minerals

There are thousands of minerals, but only about 200 are common in rocks. Sedimentary rocks are often made of mostly one mineral. For example, limestone is made from ancient seashells, so it's mostly composed of the chemical compound calcium carbonate. It forms the metamorphic rock marble, so marble is also mainly calcium carbonate. Sandstone is made from compacted sand, which is silicon dioxide—a compound of the two most common elements in Earth's crust. Heat and pressure turn sandstone into the metamorphic rock quartzite.

Pumice is foamed, igneous rock. It erupted from a volcano like soda from a shaken bottle, then cooled quickly, leaving holes where the gas bubbles had been.

The sandstone of this formation has been shaped by rain and wind. The weathering reveals the strata, or the lines and ridges that show the layers of rock in the formation.

Around 150 million years ago, this rock would have been a huge sand dune. Over time, winds blew the sand into layers of different grain sizes.

Eventually, the sand in this dune compacted into stone. The waving colors are a result of the iron, manganese, and other mineral salts in water that have seeped through the porous sandstone.

DID YOU KNOW? Earth's oldest rocks are igneous faux amphibolites in Canada. At 4.28 billion years old, they were probably once part of Earth's earliest crust.

Wonderful Water

Water is Earth's superpower! Our planet is just the right distance from the sun for liquid water to exist. Without water, life on Earth could not happen, because living cells and biochemical reactions can occur only with water. Luckily, Earth recycles our precious water so none of it is lost.

Water molecules freeze into six-sided crystals. The six arms of a snow crystal are built up from a tiny, six-sided plate of frozen water vapor.

The Water Cycle

When a puddle dries up, the water isn't lost. It has just evaporated. The sun's heat has changed it into water vapor, much like it does to the molecules at the surface of seas, lakes, and rivers. This vapor rises, cools, and condenses into droplets inside clouds. The droplets get heavier until they fall as precipitation. The liquid water falls on land and flows into rivers or seeps through rocks to eventually collect in the sea.

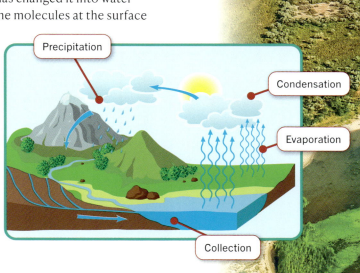

Precipitation · Condensation · Evaporation · Collection

HALL OF FAME

Chandrasekhara Venkata Raman
1888–1970

Chandrasekhara Venkata Raman was an Indian physicist who won the Nobel Prize in physics in 1930 for his work in spectroscopy and the scattering of light. He described water as the elixir of life after standing on the edge of the desert beside the Nile valley in Egypt and seeing the difference between the empty desert sand and the fertile land by the river, where life thrived.

The Danube River splits to form a fan-shaped area of swampy land along the coastline called a delta.

An estuary is where a river meets the sea. The fresh water of the river mingles with the seawater, so estuaries have brackish water that's slightly salty.

Sediment carried by the river is deposited in deltas and estuaries. The rich soils and the actions of the tides form unique ecosystems and wildlife habitats.

The Danube River begins in Germany and touches 10 countries on its 1,770-mile (2,850-km) journey to the Black Sea.

The Very Odd Molecule

Water has many strange properties. It is a compound of hydrogen and oxygen. These atoms are so light that water should be a gas at room temperature, but instead it's a liquid. When it freezes, we'd expect it to become denser, but instead it expands. So, ice floats instead of sinking. Water molecules also tend to stick to one another, which allows trees to draw water up their tall trunks against gravity.

Water striders can walk on water because water molecules stick together. This cohesion creates surface tension that the insect is too light to break through.

DID YOU KNOW? Water once flowed on the surface of Mars, and scientists think there's still liquid water underground. That could mean there was once life on Mars.

Creative Carbon

Carbon is the fundamental element of life. It can make anything from a microbe to a whale by bonding with atoms of other elements, such as hydrogen, oxygen, and nitrogen. Carbon acts like a backbone, stringing all these atoms together into long, strong molecules that make the carbohydrates, proteins, and fats that build and sustain living things.

Chemical Factories

Plants are natural chemical factories. They absorb carbon dioxide—a compound of carbon and oxygen—from the air and use this gas alongside water to make the sugar glucose and the gas oxygen. This process is called photosynthesis. In turn, the glucose molecules make bigger carbohydrates that build the plant's body. Humans are chemical factories, too! When we eat a plant or an animal, we use its carbon and other atoms to make proteins that build our bodies and give us energy. The chemical instructions for these processes are kept in long molecules called DNA, which are packed into every cell in our bodies.

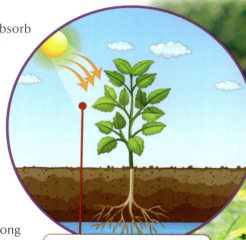

Photosynthesis creates glucose, a molecule with 6 oxygen and 12 hydrogen atoms on a chain of 6 carbon atoms.

Coal, gas, and oil are the remains of plants and animals that died millions of years ago. Burning these fossil fuels releases carbon dioxide into the atmosphere.

The Carbon Cycle

Living things return their carbon atoms to the environment in different ways. Carbon dioxide is made during respiration—a process that makes energy—and leaves the body as you breathe out. Carbon is also released by rotting plants and from the bodies of dead animals. Organisms in the soil called decomposers help this waste break down into simple chemicals that plants can absorb. These decomposers also release carbon dioxide into the air during respiration. Plants take in carbon dioxide to make sugars, and the carbon cycle goes on.

HALL OF FAME

Jan Baptista van Helmont
1580—1644

In 1634, Belgian chemist Jan Baptista van Helmont planted a young willow tree in a pot of soil. After five years, the tree was 30 times heavier, but the soil's weight had hardly changed. This experiment showed that the plant was getting nutrients from somewhere other than the soil, and it helped later scientists discover the process of photosynthesis.

Think of trees and people as a team! Trees make oxygen for us to breathe, and we make carbon dioxide for them to use in photosynthesis.

When trees photosynthesize, they lock carbon into their branches and roots. This reduces carbon dioxide in the atmosphere and helps control global warming.

Plants contain chlorophyll, a green pigment that absorbs energy from sunlight.

DID YOU KNOW? More than half of your body weight is water. If you take away the water, half of what's left is carbon.

Essential Oxygen

Many living things need oxygen for respiration. The gas makes up around 21 percent of Earth's atmosphere. Like other chemicals widely used in biological processes, oxygen is never used up but keeps being recycled through the environment.

The Element

Oxygen is the third most abundant element in the universe, after hydrogen and helium. It's the most common element in Earth's crust, mostly combined with silicon. And it is also the most common element in the human body. Pure oxygen has no color, smell, or taste. It reacts readily with other elements to make compounds called oxides. Oxides are everywhere. Water is an oxide of hydrogen, sand is an oxide of silicon, and rust is an oxide of iron.

Oxidation is the addition of oxygen atoms to chemicals. An apple goes brown after it is cut and exposed to air because of an oxidation reaction.

The Oxygen Cycle

Plants on land and sea drive the oxygen cycle through photosynthesis. They release oxygen into the air, which animals use for breathing, or respiration. Respiration turns glucose and oxygen into carbon dioxide and water. At the same time, energy is released, which animals use for chemical reactions in their cells.

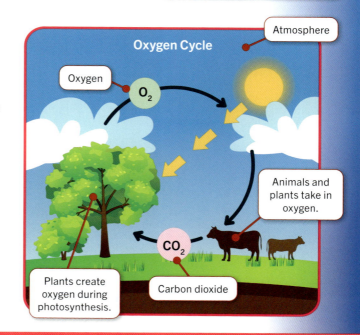

DID YOU KNOW? Giant dragonflies lived 300 million years ago, when higher oxygen levels allowed insects to grow very large.

Many land animals breathe air and oxygen into their lungs, but fish get oxygen by taking water into their mouths and passing it over feathery gills.

Tiny organisms in the sea called cyanobacteria started to produce oxygen through photosynthesis about 2.5 billion years ago, and so began to add oxygen to Earth's atmosphere.

Oxygen moves from seawater into blood vessels in the gills. It's carried by the blood to the rest of the fish's body, where respiration happens.

Respiration with oxygen is called aerobic respiration. Anaerobic respiration occurs without oxygen. Our muscle cells go through anaerobic respiration during heavy exercise.

HALL OF FAME

Joseph Priestley
1733–1804

Carl Wilhelm Scheele produced oxygen in Sweden in 1771, but he did not publish his discovery until six years later. Meanwhile, English scientist Joseph Priestley published his discovery of oxygen in 1774, after collecting the gas that was produced from mercuric oxide heated by sunlight. Priestley found that the gas made breathing easier and made a candle burn more brightly.

Team Nitrogen

Nitrogen makes up most of Earth's atmosphere. Living things need the element to make proteins, but there's a problem. Nitrogen atoms in the air bond together strongly in pairs, and these bonds must be broken before the nitrogen atoms can form other compounds. Luckily, a team of soil bacteria helps break nitrogen atoms apart so living things can use them.

The Nitrogen Cycle

Nitrogen-fixing bacteria recycle nitrogen in the environment. These bacteria separate the N_2 atoms so they can combine in compounds called nitrates. This is called nitrogen fixing. The nitrates are absorbed by plants and used to make proteins. Nitrogen atoms pass through the food chain until they return to the soil in plant and animal waste or in decomposing bodies. Then, different bacteria recycle them into either nitrates in the soil or pure nitrogen in the air.

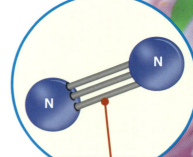

Nitrogen atoms can make three bonds, so two atoms link up with very strong triple bonds. This makes the unreactive molecule N_2.

Lightning, volcanoes, and fires also fix nitrogen by breaking apart the N_2 molecules, allowing the free nitrogen atoms to combine with other elements.

Haber Process

The Haber process is an industrial method that fixes nitrogen by turning nitrogen gas and hydrogen into ammonia (NH_3). The ammonia is made into nitrogen-based fertilizers such as ammonium nitrate, which help farm crops grow. However, overuse of fertilizers can put too much nitrate into rivers and streams and upset the natural nitrogen cycle. Alternative methods of adding nitrates to soils are rotating crops with nitrogen-fixing plants, such as legumes, as well as the use of manure and other natural fertilizers.

DID YOU KNOW? Early Egyptian alchemists made sal ammoniac (ammonium chloride) for smelling salts by heating dung and urine with salt.

Farmers enrich their fields by planting clover. Nitrogen-fixing bacteria in the clover roots turn nitrogen from the air into nitrates.

Some nitrates in the soil are converted back into N_2 in the air by denitrifying bacteria.

Decomposers and nitrifying bacteria break down the waste from living and dead animals and plants, making more nitrates available.

Nitrogen-fixing bacteria form nodules on the clover roots, where nitrates build up. The clover uses the nitrates, and animals then eat the clover to gain the nitrogen.

HALL OF FAME

**Samuel Massie
1919–2005**

Distinguished chemist Samuel Massie went to Agricultural Mechanical Normal College after being prevented from going to the University of Arkansas because he was Black. His research included developing agents to protect soldiers from poisonous gases, investigating how pollution from ships affects sea life, and studying nitrogen and sulfur compounds for treating infectious diseases.

Crucial Glucose

Every living thing is constantly building up and breaking down molecules. All these chemical reactions together form a creature's metabolism. Glucose is particularly important in metabolism. It's a monosaccharide, or a simple sugar made of just one molecule.

Getting Glucose

Plants use energy from the sun to make glucose from carbon dioxide and water. They use the glucose to make bigger molecules, such as cellulose and starch. As animals, we get glucose from plants when we eat starchy foods, such as bread, rice, and potatoes. During digestion, our bodies break these starches down into simple sugars, which our blood carries to our tissues. There, tiny cell structures release energy from the molecules to use in cell processes.

Very few living things can survive in the depths of the ocean around deep-sea hydrothermal vents. However, some bacteria can thrive by making glucose from the hydrogen sulfide and methane released by these undersea vents.

Green parts of plants absorb sunlight and trap its energy in glucose molecules during photosynthesis. Energy is stored in the bonds between atoms that make up glucose molecules.

HALL OF FAME

Marie Maynard Daly
1921–2003

Marie Maynard Daly was the first Black woman to earn a PhD in chemistry in the United States. Her studies focused on the role of enzymes in starch digestion and the structure and biochemical activities of the cell nucleus. Daly taught biochemistry and became a professor at the Albert Einstein College of Medicine. She also pushed to enroll more minority students in medical and scientific studies.

Making Polysaccharides

Monosaccharides join up in chains to make long natural polymers called polysaccharides. Glucose molecules ($C_6H_{12}O_6$) link up to make polysaccharides, such as starch and cellulose. As each glucose molecule links up, a water molecule (H_2O) is lost, so the polysaccharide formula is $(C_6H_{10}O_5)_n$, where *n* means any number of repeated molecules. Starch is a molecule used to store energy. Cellulose is used to build strong structures, such as those that make up tree trunks.

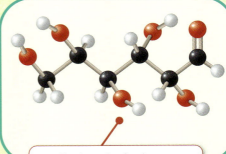

The formula of a glucose molecule is $C_6H_{12}O_6$ because it has 6 carbon atoms, 12 hydrogen atoms, and 6 oxygen atoms.

Glucose can be stored, used to release energy from food molecules, or used to make larger molecules to grow a plant's body.

Glucose is stored as starch in leaves, stems, roots, seeds, and fruit. The energy-giving, digestible nutrients we get from starchy foods are called carbohydrates.

DID YOU KNOW? The human brain accounts for around 2 percent of our weight, but it uses around 20 percent of the glucose energy needed by the body.

Plant Chemicals

Plants and fungi don't seem to do much, but in fact they're busy doing amazing chemistry! There are chemical reactions going on inside them all the time. Plants have the important job of trapping energy and making glucose to build their bodies through photosynthesis. But the chemicals of photosynthesis aren't the only ones involved in a plant's everyday life.

Plant Hormones

Plants need light, and they often seek it out. They have hormones, or chemical messengers, called auxins that control the growth of their root and shoot tips. Auxins in shoot tips move away from light. They concentrate in the shadiest side of shoots and make the cells there grow faster, so the shoots bend toward the light. Auxins in root tips diffuse downward in response to gravity. This makes the cells grow more slowly on the underside of the tips, so the roots grow down.

Leaves contain red and yellow pigments, which act as sunscreen. They're hidden by the green pigment chlorophyll, so we usually see these pigments only in the fall when trees stop producing chlorophyll.

Wood Wide Web

Trees look solitary, but they share food and chemical messages as a community. Threads of fungi called hyphae link the tree roots underground, making a network called the wood wide web. The fungi get glucose from the trees and give nutrients in return, and they make a pathway for trees to share nutrients. Older trees feed sugars to seedlings, while less friendly trees send harmful chemicals. Plants are also able to know when other plants close to them are being eaten, and they respond by making protective chemicals in their own leaves.

Most of a fungus's body is hidden underground. Fungi aren't plants, so they don't photosynthesize. They break down decaying material to get to the nutrients inside.

DID YOU KNOW? The Venus flytrap can count! When an insect touches its sensory hairs, the plant counts two touches before snapping its trap shut.

HALL OF FAME

Salimuzzaman Siddiqui
1897–1994

Salimuzzaman Siddiqui was an Indian-born scientist who earned his PhD in organic chemistry in Germany in 1927. He studied traditional herbal therapies, isolating Indian snakeroot alkaloids, which are used as sedatives and in treating high blood pressure. Siddiqui also extracted compounds from neem tree oil to treat infections. As a chemistry professor at Karachi University, he did much to advance science in Pakistan.

Many plants contain poisonous chemicals to discourage munching. Ragwort is a British wildflower that contains toxic chemicals called alkaloids.

Cinnabar moth caterpillars feed on ragwort. The plant's toxins don't hurt them. Instead, they stay in the caterpillars' bodies, making them poisonous, too.

Ragwort can harm farm animals if they eat a lot of it, but it supplies nectar and pollen to many insects.

Body Chemistry

Out of the millions of chemicals on Earth, just a few organic, carbon-based compounds are used by living organisms. These biomolecules include proteins, carbohydrates, lipids, and nucleic acids. Animal bodies are built from these molecules, and the chemical reactions that involve them are known as metabolism.

Proteins

Proteins are polymers, or long-chain molecules, made of amino acids. There are around 20,000 different proteins in your body, including hemoglobin, which carries oxygen in red blood cells. Your muscles work because proteins contract and slide over one another. Enzymes that break down your food, such as adrenaline and insulin, are proteins. So are chemical messengers called hormones. Nucleic acids, found in chromosomes, are not proteins, but they are the chemicals that carry the code to make proteins.

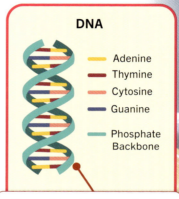

DNA
- Adenine
- Thymine
- Cytosine
- Guanine
- Phosphate Backbone

The nucleic acid DNA carries the code for making proteins in a long chain of four compounds—adenine, thymine, cytosine, and guanine. This code is passed on to offspring.

Skeletons

Skeletons are hard structures that protect animals' soft tissues, hold them up, and help them move. Animals with backbones have a bony, inner skeleton made of a protein called collagen strengthened with calcium phosphate. Many invertebrates have skeletons outside their bodies. An insect's exoskeleton acts like a suit of armor made of a polymer called chitin, while snails and other mollusks build shells out of calcium carbonate.

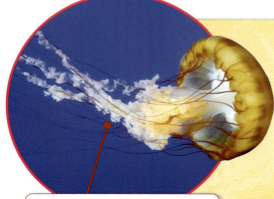

Jellyfish are 95 percent water! The water pressure gives their bodies shape, and they squirt it out one way to move in the opposite direction.

DID YOU KNOW? Your smile shows off the hardest compound in your body—tooth enamel. This compound is made of a calcium phosphate crystal called hydroxyapatite.

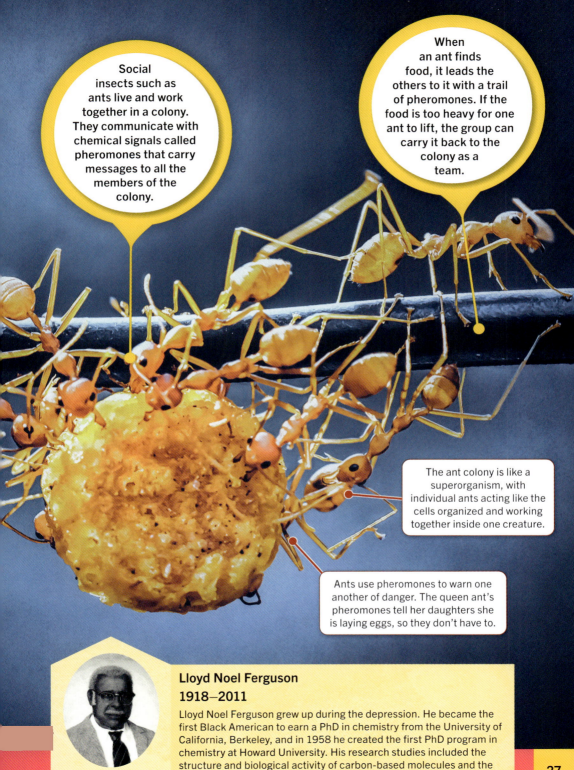

Chemists in the Lab

While chemistry happens everywhere, most chemists do their research in labs equipped with special scientific equipment that helps the scientists study, combine, and separate chemicals. There is also often safety equipment that helps chemists handle dangerous chemicals. Many high schools, universities, and even professional research laboratories are equipped with similar things.

Alchemy

Before there was chemistry, many people in ancient Asia, Africa, and Europe studied alchemy. The main goal of alchemy was to find the secret to turning base metals, such as copper, aluminum, and iron, into gold using simple chemical reactions. Scientists now know that this is impossible. But in the process of searching for this secret, alchemists made many discoveries and created many tools that chemists use today.

The Chemist's Toolbox

One of the most common tools found in a chemistry lab is the Bunsen burner. This piece of equipment burns gas to create a flame that can heat chemicals and sterilize equipment. A centrifuge can separate the components that make up a liquid. Advanced tools, such as digital microscopes and mass spectrometers, can identify the elements in a substance or measure the mass of a microscopic molecule.

A centrifuge

DID YOU KNOW? Some scientists today use artificial intelligence to assist in making discoveries. AI helped two scientists win the 2024 Nobel Prize in Chemistry.

Fume hoods pull air up and out of the lab. This helps ensure proper ventilation, protecting scientists from dangerous gases released by certain chemical reactions.

To make sure they are adding just the right amount of each chemical in an experiment, scientists use tools called pipettes.

Chemists often work with hazardous chemicals, such as acids, flammable materials, or explosives. They wear safety goggles and lab coats to protect themselves during experiments.

Dorothy Hodgkin
1910–1994

Dorothy Hodgkin was a chemist who spent her life researching the structures of biochemical molecules, despite developing painful rheumatoid arthritis at a young age. She won the Nobel Prize for Chemistry in 1964 after discovering the atomic structures of penicillin and vitamin B_{12} using X-ray crystallography. She is the only British woman to have received a science Nobel Prize.

HALL OF FAME

Reagents

Carbohydrates, fats, vitamins, and proteins are part of our diet, and food tests show which of them are in which foods. We can use reagents, or chemicals that detect other chemicals, to do this. The tests can be as simple as adding a reagent to a food sample in a test tube and observing the color changes.

Sudden Clouds and Disappearing Blue

Lipids are fats and oils found in things like butter and cream. Scientists identify them with an emulsion test by adding ethanol to a food sample in a test tube and shaking it, then pouring it into water. If lipids are present, the liquid turns cloudy. The test for vitamin C, commonly found in fruit, uses the dark blue reagent dichlorophenolindophenol (DCPIP). A sample is added to the DCPIP drop by drop while the mixture is being shaken. If vitamin C is present, the color vanishes.

An electric water bath warms a sample to a set temperature without overheating it, but a beaker of hot water works just as well.

Changing Colors

Benedict's and biuret reagents are both bright blue solutions. Benedict's solution tests for sugars, such as glucose. It's added to a sample, and the test tube is warmed gently in a water bath. The liquid changes through a series of shades if sugar is present. The biuret test is for proteins. Two reagents—copper sulfate and sodium hydroxide—are added to the food sample. If protein is present, the blue mixture turns purple.

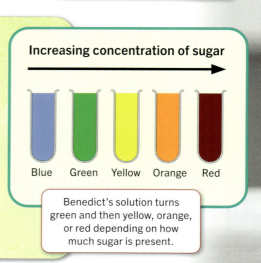

Increasing concentration of sugar

Blue   Green   Yellow   Orange   Red

Benedict's solution turns green and then yellow, orange, or red depending on how much sugar is present.

DID YOU KNOW? A person eating 10 carrots every day might see their palms turn orange, due to a large amount of the pigment beta-carotene.

The test for starch is a yellow-brown iodine solution. It turns blue-black in the presence of starch.

The iodine reaction happens only with starch, so we know it's not detecting sugars or other carbohydrates.

Fruits lose starch as they ripen. Some orchards use iodine tests to find the ripeness of their apples by measuring how much starch is left.

HALL OF FAME

Robert Boyle
1627–1691

Irish-born Robert Boyle was the first leading scientist to carry out controlled experiments and publish the results with details about procedure, apparatus, and observation. He is most famous for Boyle's Law concerning the volume and pressure of gases, but he also introduced many standard chemical tests.

Acid and Alkali Tests

Chemicals called acids in your stomach help you digest food. On the pH scale, which measures acidity and alkalinity, acids score between pH 0 and pH 6, with pH 0 being the strongest. Stomach acids score a powerful pH 1! Alkalies score between pH 8 and pH 14 on the scale. While they are found at opposite ends of the scale, strong solutions of either acids or alkalies can damage materials and living tissues.

When universal indicator paper is dipped into a solution, it changes to a shade that can be matched with a reference to the pH scale.

Indicators

The stronger the acid, the more damage it can do. Chemists test solutions for acidity and alkalinity with indicators. Litmus paper is dipped into a solution and shows if it is acidic by turning red or alkaline by turning blue. Universal indicator tells us how strongly acidic or alkaline a solution is by changing to a range of shades. Universal indicator comes as strips of paper for dipping or as a liquid for mixing into a test solution.

Neutralization

Acids and alkalies neutralize each other. They react to form a salt and water. Both the salt and the water are pH 7, or neutral. The reaction between hydrochloric acid and alkaline sodium hydroxide produces a salt called sodium chloride, which is table salt. Most salts are not table salt, and the name of the salt depends on the acid that produced it. For example, the reaction between sulfuric acid and copper oxide makes copper sulfate.

Titration tests how much alkali neutralizes an acid. An alkali is added slowly until the point where the universal indicator liquid in the mixture shows that it has become neutral.

DID YOU KNOW? Rainwater is naturally around pH 6, but polluted acid rain has been measured at pH 2. That's as acidic as a lemon!

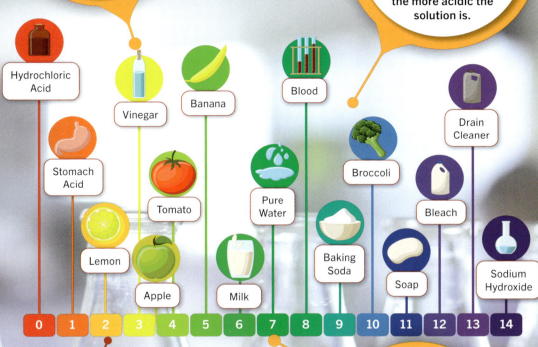

If you soak an egg in vinegar for a day, the acidic vinegar dissolves the eggshell, leaving a rubbery, bouncy egg.

The term *pH* means potential of hydrogen. Dissolved acids add positively charged hydrogen ions (H^+) to a solution. The more hydrogen ions there are, the more acidic the solution is.

Citrus fruits, such as lemons and limes, contain citric acid. They can damage tooth enamel, so they're best eaten at mealtimes alongside other foods that balance their pH.

The pH scale goes from highly acidic 0 to highly alkaline 14. pH 7 is neutral. Pure water is pH 7, so it's neither acidic nor alkaline.

Soren Sorensen
1868–1939

Danish scientist Soren Sorensen was the director of chemistry at the Carlsberg Laboratory in Copenhagen, Denmark. With his wife, Margrethe, he studied the effect of ion concentration in protein analysis and found that enzymes work best at certain acid or alkali levels. In 1909, he introduced the pH scale as a simple way of describing the acidity of solutions.

HALL OF FAME

33

Acid Reactions

Acids are corrosive, meaning they can burn skin, damage materials, and even dissolve metals. So, it's very important to follow safety procedures, such as wearing eye protection, when handling acids in laboratory experiments.

Acids and Metals

Acids react with metals to make hydrogen and a metal compound called a salt. The metal takes the place of hydrogen in the solution, and the displaced hydrogen is released as bubbles of gas. The equation for these reactions is acid + metal ⟶ salt + hydrogen. For example: sulfuric acid + zinc ⟶ zinc sulfate + hydrogen.

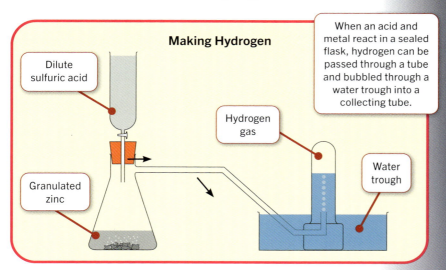

Making Hydrogen

- Dilute sulfuric acid
- Granulated zinc
- Hydrogen gas
- Water trough

When an acid and metal react in a sealed flask, hydrogen can be passed through a tube and bubbled through a water trough into a collecting tube.

HALL OF FAME

Henry Cavendish
1731–1810

Henry Cavendish was a French physicist and chemist. He made the first attempt to calculate the weight of Earth. His measurement was off by only 10 percent! He studied the properties of the gas given off when a metal and acid reacted, and so discovered hydrogen in 1766.

DID YOU KNOW? The word *acid* comes from the Latin word for sour. Many fruits are sour because they contain strong acids.

Acids and Metal Oxides

Metals react with oxygen to form oxides—compounds that contain oxygen. Metal oxides make alkaline solutions, and so are basic rather than acidic. Alkalies react with acids to neutralize one another, resulting in products of pH 7. So, the reaction of an acid with a metal oxide is a neutralization reaction. It produces a salt plus water. For example:
sulfuric acid + zinc oxide ⟶ zinc sulfate + water.

Zinc sulfate is used in fertilizers and in medicines as a zinc supplement. Zinc is a trace element needed in small amounts by all living things.

The reactivity series lists metals from most to least reactive. The most reactive ones explode in dilute acids, while the least reactive don't react at all. Those in the middle bubble gently.

Iron is in the middle of the reactivity series. It reacts to dilute hydrochloric acid, but it doesn't do so violently.

35

Fire and Flame Tests

We can learn a lot about chemicals by burning them. Some metal salts burn with colorful flames at very high temperatures. This happens because the salts contain positively charged ions. Different metal ions produce different flame colors.

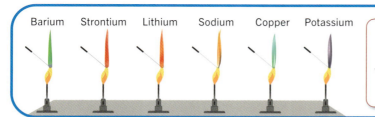

Ion identification by flame reveals barium with a green color, strontium and lithium with red, sodium with yellow, copper with blue-green, and potassium with lilac.

A Bunsen burner

Flame Tests for Metals

A Bunsen burner can be adjusted to burn hotter by mixing more air with the gas as it burns. The hottest flame is roaring blue—a noisy, almost invisible flame. This is the flame setting used to test metals. The scientist dips a wire loop in a sample of a metal salt and then holds it in the flame. The color that the flame turns reveals the type of metal salt being tested.

Splint Tests for Gases

Oxygen, hydrogen, and carbon dioxide gases are commonly given off in laboratory experiments. One way to identify these invisible gases is with a lighted splint, a long and thin piece of wood. A lighted splint makes an explosive squeaky pop when it's inserted into a test tube full of hydrogen, and it goes out in a tube of carbon dioxide.

A glowing splint—one that has been lit and then blown out so that it has no flame—will burst into fire in the presence of oxygen.

DID YOU KNOW? Carbon dioxide does not burn easily. It is used in many fire extinguishers.

Fireworks contain fuel, such as charcoal, plus metals and metal salts to make vivid colors. Oxidizing chemicals, such as nitrates, provide oxygen to make them burn more brightly.

Blue firework colors are the hardest to produce, because copper salts break down at very high temperatures.

Aluminum and magnesium make bright white and silvery sparks.

Fireworks manufacturers mix different metals to get even more colors. A mixture of strontium and copper salts makes purple.

HALL OF FAME

Li Tian
Seventh Century

In around 650 CE, a Chinese monk named Li Tian is said to have experimented with sulfur, potassium nitrate, and honey. He stuffed the resulting mixture into bamboo shoots, which exploded in the fire, becoming the first fireworks. Gunpowder was probably invented later, when charcoal was added to the mix.

Spectra

There's a rainbow inside sunlight. The colors are combined, so it looks like colorless white light. Light energy travels in waves. When we see different colored light, we're seeing waves of different lengths. For example, blue light has a shorter wavelength than red light.

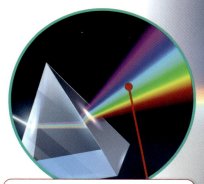

When light passes through certain transparent objects, such as raindrops or a prism, the wavelengths bend and spread into a rainbow. A rainbow is one type of spectrum.

Absorption and Emission Spectra

Atoms absorb and emit specific colors of light. Very hot objects, such as stars, produce white light. When this white light shines through a cold gas, the elements in the gas absorb some of the colors. This creates an absorption spectrum with dark stripes where light has been removed. The colors of the missing light tell us which elements are in the gas. A cloud of hot gas produces a few colors of light. This is the emission spectrum, and the colors also show what gas is in the cloud.

This pattern of stripes in the absorption and emission spectra is clearly indicating the presence of oxygen.

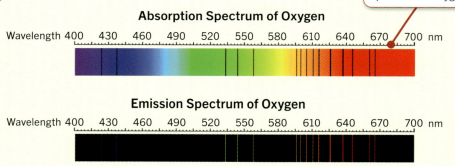

HALL OF FAME

Alma Levant Hayden
1927–1967

Alma Levant Hayden was a Black American chemist. She was an expert in spectrometry and led the team that analyzed Krebiozen. This expensive chemical was sold as a wonder drug for treating cancer, but Hayden showed it was a useless fake. Hayden became head of the spectrophotometer research branch of the Pharmaceutical Chemistry Division of the FDA in 1963.

Objects reflect certain wavelengths, and they absorb other shades of light. Leaves look green because they reflect green light and absorb the rest.

In a double rainbow, the colors in the higher rainbow are reversed.

When sunlight passes through raindrops in the sky, the light splits to form a visible light spectrum, which we call a rainbow.

When sunlight hits Earth's atmosphere, the short waves of blue light are scattered more than the other colors. So, we see a blue sky.

Mass Spectrum

A mass spectrometer is similar to a racetrack inside a magnetic field. Ions from a chemical sample race along a tube, and the magnetic field deflects them and makes them move in a curve. How much they curve depends on their mass. Lighter ions deflect more than heavier ones. The ions are detected at the end of the tube, and the results appear as a mass spectrum graph showing which elements are present and in what amounts.

This mass spectrometer analyzes chemicals in a medical lab. A sample is vaporized and ionized at the front of the instrument.

DID YOU KNOW? The longest-lasting rainbow ever recorded occurred in 2017. It stayed visible for 8 hours and 58 minutes!

Chromatography

Chromatography is a beautiful example of chemical analysis. It shows what's in a sample solution by separating out the different dissolved substances. It's done with a stationary phase, such as paper, and a mobile phase, such as a liquid that travels up the paper. This process makes amazing patterns called chromatograms.

Paper Chromatography

Paper chromatography uses absorbent paper to separate colored solutions. It works well for inks or dyes. Paper marked with a dot of ink is placed in a beaker of water, so the dot is above the waterline. The water travels up the paper. It reaches the dot and continues upward, carrying the ink with it. Some of the substances in the ink go farther up the paper than others, so a pattern appears above the original dot.

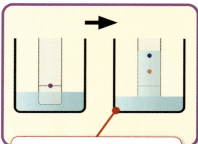

A dye with two components would make a chromatogram like this. A pure substance would make a pattern of just one color.

Gas chromatography is used to analyze urine samples from athletes to see if they have taken banned substances to help them win.

Gas Chromatography

Gas chromatography is used to separate complex mixtures. The mobile phase is a carrier gas, such as helium. The stationary phase is a solid, such as silica, packed into a tube. The gas carries the sample, which separates into its parts as it travels along the column. A computer displays the gas chromatogram as a graph showing how many substances, and how much of them, are in the sample.

DID YOU KNOW? Chromatography has shown that people living in Peru 6,000 years ago were already making indigo dye, which is used to dye blue jeans today.

Learning from Nature

From the earliest chemists of the ancient world to the research chemists making new discoveries in labs all around the planet, scientists have been inspired by the natural world to help solve the toughest challenges through chemistry. With the help of new tools in their labs, chemists have created life-saving medicines, helped farmers grow larger crops, and helped protect endangered ecosystems. These scientists know that there is still so much more to learn about chemistry, both in nature and in the lab.

Chemistry in Medicine

Many recent discoveries in medicine have been made by chemists. Geneticists, or scientists who study the chemistry of DNA, have learned how to make medicines that treat specific illnesses rather than symptoms. Some chemists hope to be able to remove or change certain sequences in DNA to make plants that can better survive climate change.

Chemists Helping the Planet

By burning fossil fuels in cars and airplanes, we create lots of carbon dioxide, a gas that contributes to global warming. Recently, chemists have been creating synthetic fuels in labs that turn carbon dioxide into energy. This could help limit the amount of carbon dioxide in the atmosphere and slow down global warming.

Review and Reflect

Now that you've read about chemistry in the lab and nature, let's review what you've learned. Use the following questions to reflect on your newfound knowledge and integrate it with what you already knew.

Check for Understanding

1. What are melting and boiling points? Why are they important to chemists? *(pp. 6-7)*

2. Explain how the big bang theory led to the formation of the elements in the universe. *(pp. 8-9)*

3. List the layers of Earth. Which one do we live on? *(p. 10)*

4. Describe some of the strange properties of water. *(p. 15)*

5. What is the carbon cycle? How does it connect plants and animals? *(pp. 16-17)*

6. What is an oxide? List a few examples. *(p. 18)*

7. How are polysaccharides formed? *(p. 23)*

8. What is the wood wide web? *(p. 24)*

9. List some of the important jobs that proteins do in the body. *(p. 26)*

10. What are some tools that chemists use in chemistry labs? *(pp. 28-29)*

11. How does universal indicator work? *(p. 32)*

12. What is the equation for acid-and-metal reactions? *(p. 34)*

13. What determines the different colors of fireworks? *(pp. 36-37)*

14. Describe how chemists use light to study gases. *(pp. 38-39)*

15. What are chromatograms and what do they show? *(p. 40)*

Making Connections

1. Choose two of the following essential chemicals to compare and contrast: water, carbon, oxygen, nitrogen, and glucose.

2. Describe all the steps for one of Earth's cycles that was outlined in this book.

3. Explain how plants and animals use chemistry to build their bodies.

4. How is alchemy similar to modern chemistry? In what ways is it different?

5. What is the pH scale? Explain how it can show the difference between an acid and an alkali.

In Your Own Words

1. Describe the scientific method that all scientists follow when they do an experiment. Think of an experiment you would like to conduct and list the steps you would take to complete it.

2. There are many kinds of tests described in this book that chemists perform in the lab. Choose a test you would like to conduct and explain why it is interesting to you.

3. Which of the people in the Hall of Fame sidebars did you find most interesting and why? How was their work important?

4. Which chemistry tool seems the most useful to you? What kind of experiment could you conduct using that tool?

5. Identify some of the chemical reactions you see on a daily basis. Are there reactions you can think of that are not mentioned in this book? List them and try to figure out what kind of chemicals are involved.

45

Glossary

acid a chemical with a value lower than 7 on the pH scale

alchemist an early scientist who hoped to change ordinary metals into gold

alkali a chemical with a value higher than 7 on the pH scale

atom the smallest unit of a chemical element

carbohydrates a group of organic chemicals that includes sugars and starches

chemical reaction a process in which atoms are rearranged, changing one or more substances into different substances

chlorophyll a green pigment in plants that absorbs light and turns it into chemical energy via photosynthesis

compound a pure chemical made from the atoms of more than one element

DNA deoxyribonucleic acid, a long molecule that carries instructions for the structure and function of living cells

electron a negatively charged particle found in an atom

element a chemical made of a single type of atom

fossil fuels nonrenewable energy sources that come from the remains of plants and animals that died long ago

gravity a force of attraction that exists between all items with mass

hormone a chemical messenger that controls bodily processes such as growth

ion an atom that carries an electric charge because it has lost or gained an electron

isotopes forms of an element with different numbers of neutrons

mineral a naturally occurring inorganic solid with a defined chemical structure

molecule a group of two or more atoms that are chemically bonded

nucleus the center part of an atom, made of protons and neutrons

respiration the process living things use to release energy

Read More

Dingle, Adrian. *My Book of the Elements (My Book).* New York: DK Publishing, 2024.

Eason, Sarah. *Minerals (The Rock Cycle Road Trip).* Minneapolis: Lerner Publications, 2025.

Jackson, Tom. *Matter & Energy (The World of Physics).* Minneapolis: Bearport Publishing Company, 2025.

McKenzie, Precious. *The Micro World of Atoms and Molecules (Micro Science).* North Mankato, MN: Capstone Press, 2022.

Learn More Online

1. Go to **FactSurfer.com** or scan the QR code below.
2. Enter **"Chemistry Lab Nature"** into the search box.
3. Click on the cover of this book to see a list of websites.

47

Index

acids 26, 29, 31–35
alchemy 12, 28
alkalies 31–32
big bang 8
bonds 20, 22
Bunsen burners 36
chemical reactions 18, 22, 24, 26, 28–29
chromatography 40–41
condensation 14
crops 20, 42
DNA (deoxyribonucleic acid) 16, 26, 42
energy 4, 8, 16–18, 22–24, 38, 43
evaporation 14
experiments 6, 12, 29, 31, 34, 36
explosions 8
fertilizers 5, 20, 35
fireworks 37
food 20, 23–24, 26–27, 30, 32
fossil fuels 16, 43
global warming 17, 43
glucose 4, 16, 18, 22–24, 30
medicines 6, 35, 42
metabolism 22, 26
metals 28, 34–37
pH 32–33, 35
photosynthesis 4, 16–19, 22, 24
plants 4–5, 16, 18, 20–22, 24–25, 42

polymers 23, 26
reactions 14, 18, 22, 24, 26, 28–29, 34
reagents 30
rocks and minerals 10–14
salt 6, 20, 32, 34–36
seas and oceans 10, 14
snow 14
soil 16–17, 20–21
solutions 30, 32–33, 35, 40
spectra 38
stars 8–9, 11, 38
substances 4, 40
sunlight 4, 17, 19, 22, 38–39
temperature 7, 11, 15, 30
thermometers 7
volcanoes 12, 20